U.S. Department of Justice
Office of Justice Programs
Bureau of Justice Statistics

June 2016, NCJ 249849

Background Checks for Firearm Transfers, 2013–14 - Statistical Tables

Jennifer C. Karberg
Ronald J. Frandsen
Joseph M. Durso
Trent D. Buskirk, Ph.D.
Regional Justice Information Service
Allina D. Lee
Bureau of Justice Statistics

More than 180 million applications for firearm transfers or permits were subject to background checks since the effective date of the Brady Handgun Violence Prevention Act on February 28, 1994, through December 31, 2014. During this period, about 2.8 million applications (1.6%) were denied. In 2014, nearly 15 million applications were subject to background checks, and 193,000 (1.3%) were denied, including about 91,000 denied by the FBI and about 102,000 denied by state and local agencies.

Data in this report were obtained from the Bureau of Justice Statistics' (BJS) Firearm Inquiry Statistics (FIST) program. The FIST program collects information on firearm applications and denials and combines this information with the FBI's National Instant Criminal Background Check System (NICS) transaction data to produce an estimated number of background checks for firearm transfers or permits since the effective date of the Brady Act.

These statistical tables describe trends in background check activities that occurred in 2014 and include partial data for 2013. Data include the number of firearm transaction applications processed by the FBI and by state and local agencies, the number of applications denied, reasons for denial, and estimates of applications by jurisdiction and by each type of approval system.

Summary findings

- Since the effective date of the Brady Act on February 28, 1994, through December 31, 2014, more than 180 million applications for firearm transfers or permits were subject to background checks. More than 2.8 million applications (1.6%) were denied (**table 1**).

- Nearly 15 million applications for firearm transfers were received in 2014, down from an estimated 17.6 million in 2013.

- About 1.3% of the nearly 15 million applications for firearm transfers or permits in 2014 were denied—about 91,000 by the FBI and about 102,000 by state and local agencies. An estimated 193,000 applications for firearm transfers or permits in 2013 were denied—about 88,000 by the FBI and about 104,000 by state and local agencies (**table 2**).

- Among state agencies, denial rates in 2014 were 3.1% for purchase permits, 1.5% for instant checks, 0.9% for other approval checks, and 1.0% for exempt carry permits. Denial rates in 2013 were estimated to be 1.9% for purchase permits, 1.2% for instant checks, 0.8% for other approval checks, and 0.9% for exempt carry permits (**table 3**).

- Among local agencies, the denial rates in 2014 were 4% for purchase permit checks and 1.2% for exempt carry permit checks (**table 4**).

- A felony conviction (42%) was the most common reason for the FBI to deny an application in 2014, followed by a fugitive from justice status (19%) (**table 5**).

Bureau of Justice Statistics • **Statistical Tables**

- Among the 18 state agencies that reported reasons for denial, a state law prohibition (26%) was the most common reason to deny an application in 2014, followed by a felony conviction (22%).

- Excluding other prohibitions, of the approximately 330 local agencies that reported reasons for denial, a state law prohibition (20%) was the most common reason to deny an application in 2014.

- Among all agencies that reported reasons for denial in 2014, denial of an application due to a felony conviction, indictment, charge, or arrest accounted for approximately 42% of denials (table 6).

- Bureau of Alcohol, Tobacco, Firearms and Explosives (ATF) field offices investigated 7,978 NICS denials that were referred by the FBI in 2014—up from 6,257 in 2013. Among denials, a felony conviction was the most common reason for referral to a field office in 2014 (37%) and in 2013 (33%) (table 7).

Tables

Appendix tables

Background

The Brady Handgun Violence Prevention Act of 1993 (Pub. L. No. 103-159, 107 Stat. 1536 (1993), codified as amended at 18 U.S.C. § 921 et seq.) mandates that a criminal history background check be performed on any person who attempts to purchase a firearm from a Federal Firearms Licensee (FFL). The permanent provisions of the Brady Act established the NICS, which the FBI or a state Point of Contact (POC) accesses prior to approval or denial of a firearm transfer. The NICS is a system comprised of data on persons who are prohibited from purchasing or possessing a firearm under federal or state law.

The Gun Control Act (18 U.S.C. § 922) prohibits transfer of a firearm to a person who—

- is under indictment for, or has been convicted of, a crime punishable by imprisonment for more than 1 year

- is a fugitive from justice

- is an unlawful user of, or addicted to, a controlled substance

- has been adjudicated as a mental defective or committed to a mental institution

- is an illegal alien or has been admitted to the United States under a nonimmigrant visa

- was dishonorably discharged from the U.S. Armed Forces

- has renounced U.S. citizenship

- is subject to a court order restraining him or her from harassing, stalking, or threatening an intimate partner or child

- has been convicted of a misdemeanor crime of domestic violence

- is under age 18 for long guns or under age 21 for handguns.

An FFL contacts either the FBI or a state POC to determine whether a prospective purchaser is prohibited from receiving a firearm. During 2014, the FBI conducted all NICS checks for 30 states, the District of Columbia, and U.S. territories. POC agencies, which may be statewide or local, conducted all NICS checks for 13 other states. In the remaining 7 states, POC agencies conducted NICS checks on handgun transfer applicants, and the FBI conducted checks on long gun transfer applicants. Several states require an additional background check that does not access the NICS. State laws may require a check on a permit applicant or a person who seeks to receive a firearm from an unlicensed seller. For more information on the NICS, visit the FBI's Criminal Justice Information Service (CJIS) website at http://www.fbi.gov/about-us/cjis/nics.

BJS began the FIST program in 1995 to provide national estimates of the total number of firearm applications received and denied pursuant to the Brady Act and similar state laws. The FIST program collects counts of firearm transfers and permit checks conducted by state and local agencies and combines this information with the FBI's NICS transaction data. In addition, FIST collects information on reasons for denials and law enforcement actions taken by the FBI and ATF against denied persons.

Overview of the national firearm check system

About 1,300 federal, state, and local agencies conduct background checks on persons who apply to purchase a firearm or for a permit that may be used to make a purchase.

Prospective firearm applicants must either undergo a NICS background check that has been requested by a dealer or present a state permit that ATF has qualified as an alternative to the point-of-transfer check.

ATF-qualified permits are those that—

- allow an applicant to possess, acquire, or carry a firearm

- were issued not more than 5 years earlier by the state where the transfer is to take place, after an authorized government official verified that possession of a firearm by the applicant would not be a violation of law.

All permits issued since November 29, 1998, must have included a NICS check. Many NICS-alternative permits may be used for multiple purchases while valid. State laws often provide that a permit will be revoked if the holder is convicted of an offense or otherwise becomes ineligible after receiving the permit.

NICS-alternative permit changes occurred in two states during 2013 and 2014. Alaska reinstated processing of NICS-alternative permits (called NICS exempt carry permits within the state) in 2013. West Virginia carry permits were qualified by ATF as a NICS alternative in 2014, after amendments to state laws.

Prior to transferring a firearm under the permanent Brady provisions, an FFL is required to obtain a completed Firearm Transaction Record (ATF form 4473) from the applicant. An FFL initiates a NICS check by contacting either the FBI or the state POC. Most inquiries are initiated by telephone. In 2002, the FBI added E-Check to allow FFLs to request a check electronically. The FBI or state POC queries available federal, state, local, and tribal systems and notifies the FFL that the transfer may proceed, may not proceed, or must be delayed pending further review of the applicant's record.

When an FFL initiates a NICS background check, a name and descriptor search is conducted to identify any matching records in three nationally held databases managed by the

FBI's CJIS. The following databases are searched during the background check process:

- The Interstate Identification Index (III) maintains individual criminal history records. As of January 8, 2015, the NICS accessed and searched 85,909,018 III records during a background check.[1]

- The National Crime Information Center (NCIC) contains data on persons who are the subjects of protection orders or active criminal warrants, immigration violators, and others. As of December 31, 2014, the NICS searched 5,598,974 NCIC records during a background check.

- The NICS Index, a database created specifically for the NICS, collects and maintains information contributed by federal, state, local, and tribal agencies pertaining to persons prohibited from receiving or possessing a firearm pursuant to federal and state law. Typically, the records maintained in the NICS Index are not available via the III or the NCIC. As of December 31, 2014, the NICS Index contained 12,881,223 records.

- The U.S. Immigration and Customs Enforcement (ICE) databases contain information on non-U.S. citizens who attempt to receive firearms in the United States. In 2014, the NICS Section and POC states sent 104,828 such queries to ICE. From February 2002 to December 31, 2014, ICE conducted more than 622,771 queries for the NICS.[2]

An applicant who is denied a firearm transfer or permit may appeal to the FBI or a POC. Some jurisdictions allow a further appeal to a court. A denied person who submitted a false application or has an outstanding warrant may be subject to arrest and prosecution under federal or state laws.

State and local NICS participation

Each state government determines the extent of its involvement in the NICS process. Three levels of state involvement currently exist:

- A full POC requests a NICS check on all firearm transfers originating in the state.

- A partial POC requests a NICS check on all handgun transfers. FFLs in the state are required to contact the FBI for NICS checks for long gun transfers.

[1]Data are reported through January 8, 2015, because the FBI did not run data through December 31, 2014, in the 2014 report, *National Instant Criminal Background Check System Operations*, available at https://www.fbi.gov/about-us/cjis/nics/reports/2014-operations-report. See also *Survey of State Criminal History Information Systems, 2014*, available at https://www.ncjrs.gov/pdffiles1/bjs/grants/249799.pdf.

[2]For more information about the NICS background check process, see the 2014 report, *National Instant Criminal Background Check System Operations*, available at https://www.fbi.gov/about-us/cjis/nics/reports/2014-operations-report.

TABLE 1

Estimated number of firearm applications received and denied since the effective date of the Brady Act, 1994–2014

| | Number of applications | | |
	Applications	Denials	Percent denied
Total	180,244,000	2,817,000	1.6%
Brady interim period[a]			
1994–1998	12,740,000	312,000	2.4%
Permanent Brady[b]	167,504,000	2,505,000	1.5%
1998[c]	893,000	20,000	2.2
1999	8,621,000	204,000	2.4
2000	7,753,000	153,000	2.0
2001	8,068,000	150,000	1.9
2002	7,926,000	136,000	1.7
2003	7,883,000	126,000	1.6
2004	8,133,000	126,000	1.6
2005	8,324,000	132,000	1.6
2006	8,772,000	135,000	1.6
2007	8,836,000	136,000	1.6
2008	10,131,000	147,000	1.5
2009	11,071,000	150,000	1.4
2010	10,643,000	153,000	1.5
2011[d]	12,135,000	160,000	1.3
2012	15,718,000	192,000	1.2
2013[d]	17,602,000	193,000	1.1
2014	14,993,000	193,000	1.3

Note: Counts are rounded to the nearest 1,000. Detail may not sum to total due to rounding. For more information on reporting agencies and sample design, see *Methodology*.

[a]From March 1, 1994, to November 29, 1998, background checks on applicants were conducted by state and local agencies, mainly on handgun transfers. See *Presale Handgun Checks, the Brady Interim Period, 1994–98* (NCJ 175034, BJS web, June 1999).

[b]NICS began operations in 1998. Checks on handgun and long gun transfers are conducted by the FBI and state and local agencies.

[c]November 30 to December 31, 1998, counts are from the NICS operations report for the period and may include multiple transactions for the same application.

[d]Totals for 2011 and 2013 were estimated. For more information on estimation methods, see *Methodology*.

Sources: Bureau of Justice Statistics, Firearm Inquiry Statistics program, 1996–2014; and FBI, National Instant Criminal Background Check System Transaction Statistics, 1998–2014.

- The state does not maintain a POC. FFLs are required to contact the FBI for NICS checks on all firearm transfers originating in the state.

Other uses of the NICS

In addition to NICS background checks required by the Brady Act, use of the NICS is limited to providing information to criminal justice agencies in connection with the issuance of a firearm- or explosives-related permit or license, or responding to an inquiry from ATF in connection with a civil or criminal law enforcement activity relating to federal firearm laws (28 CFR § 25.6). Firearm-related permits include ATF-qualified alternative permits and other permits issued by state or local agencies. In addition to checks on new and renewed applications, rechecks may be conducted on current permit holders.

TABLE 2
Firearm applications received and denied, by type of agency and type of check, 2013 and 2014

Type of checks conducted	2013			2014			1999–2014[a,b]		
	Applications	Denials	Percent denied	Applications	Denials	Percent denied	Applications	Denials	Percent denied
National total (FIST and FBI)	17,601,671	192,564	1.1%	14,993,408	193,363	1.3%	167,504,390	2,504,970	1.5%
FBI total	9,315,963	88,203	0.9	8,256,688	90,895	1.1	93,453,528	1,166,676	1.2
State and local total (FIST)	8,285,708	104,361	1.3	6,736,720	102,468	1.5	74,050,862	1,338,294	1.8
State agencies	7,216,496	83,477	1.2%	5,951,358	85,998	1.4%	62,723,892	1,124,194	1.8%
Instant checks[c]	4,433,318	52,866	1.2	3,757,906	56,343	1.5	41,791,852	804,830	1.9
Purchase permits[d]	699,845	13,549	1.9	412,175	12,741	3.1	6,236,277	151,300	2.4
Exempt carry permits[e]	972,147	8,299	0.9	805,185	7,878	1.0	5,838,101	79,908	1.4
Other approvals[f]	1,111,186	8,763	0.8	976,092	9,036	0.9	8,857,663	88,157	1.0
Local agencies[g]	1,069,212	20,884	2.0%	785,362	16,470	2.1%	11,326,970	214,099	1.9%
Purchase permits[d]	424,579	14,693	3.5	289,080	11,548	4.0	6,165,722	149,056	2.4
Exempt carry permits[e]	437,208	4,919	1.1	359,207	4,247	1.2	3,792,733	54,182	1.4
Other approvals[f]	207,425	1,273	0.6	137,075	675	0.5	1,368,516	10,862	0.8

[a]Includes December 1998.

[b]Includes estimates for local agencies and some state agencies in 2011 and 2013, when FIST was not collected. For details on the estimation procedure used, see *Methodology*.

[c]Require a seller to transmit a buyer's application to a checking agency by telephone or computer. The agency is required to respond immediately or as soon as possible.

[d]Require a buyer to obtain, after a background check, a government-issued document (such as a permit, license, or identification card) that must be presented to a seller before the buyer can receive a firearm.

[e]State concealed weapons permits, issued after a background check, that exempt the holder from a new check at the time of purchase under a Bureau of Alcohol, Tobacco, Firearms and Explosives ruling or state law.

[f]Require a seller to transmit an application to a checking agency, with transfers delayed until a waiting period expires or the agency completes a check.

[g]Totals were estimated. For more information, see *Methodology*.

Sources: Bureau of Justice Statistics, Firearm Inquiry Statistics program, 2013 and 2014; and FBI, National Instant Criminal Background Check System Transaction Statistics, 2013 and 2014.

TABLE 3
Firearm applications received and denied by state agencies, by type of check, 2013 and 2014

Type of check and jurisdiction	2013			2014		
	Applications	Denials	Percent denied	Applications	Denials	Percent denied
Instant check	4,433,318	52,866	1.2%	3,757,906	56,343	1.5%
Colorado	396,955	7,351	1.9	314,976	6,068	1.9
Connecticut	145,552	210	0.1	115,460	91	0.1
Florida	869,560	11,493	1.3	774,363	11,372	1.5
Illinois[a]	505,009	1,448	0.3	401,899	1,616	0.4
Nevada	120,891	1,908	1.6	95,427	1,716	1.8
New Hampshire	50,700	350	0.7	43,000	340	0.8
New Jersey	123,553	620	0.5	95,267	464	0.5
Oregon	263,283	2,151	0.8	233,878	1,590	0.7
Pennsylvania[b]	759,316	8,952	1.2	655,457	9,620	1.5
Tennessee	473,610	13,267	2.8	428,017	17,832	4.2
Utah	110,623	1,587	1.4	91,437	1,985	2.2
Virginia	479,253	2,412	0.5	405,838	2,661	0.7
Wisconsin	135,013	1,117	0.8	102,887	988	1.0
Other approval	1,111,186	8,763	0.8%	976,092	9,036	0.9%
California	960,179	7,493	0.8	931,037	8,569	0.9
Maryland	129,359	1,125	0.9	28,633	346	1.2
Rhode Island[c]	21,648	145	0.7	16,422	121	0.7
Purchase permit	699,845	13,549	1.9%	412,175	12,741	3.1%
Connecticut	55,742	60	0.1	17,904	21	0.1
District of Columbia	1,154	10	0.9	1,366	10	0.7
Hawaii[c]	22,765	232	1.0	19,365	148	0.8
Illinois[a]	324,921	6,893	2.1	170,178	7,941	4.7
Maryland	4,775	46	1.0	16,306	251	1.5
Massachusetts[c]	125,491	3,144	2.5	68,906	2,600	3.8
Michigan[c]	58,831	1,228	2.1	43,702	952	2.2
New Jersey[c]	106,166	1,936	1.8	74,448	818	1.1
Exempt carry	972,147	8,299	0.9%	805,185	7,878	1.0%
Alaska	1,774	12	0.7	2,018	12	0.6
Arizona	71,104	364	0.5	52,049	358	0.7
Arkansas	58,699	431	0.7	41,725	920	2.2
Kansas	31,004	72	0.2	21,976	146	0.7
Kentucky	58,706	1,098	1.9	31,889	560	1.8
Michigan[c]	129,900	1,662	1.3	115,601	2,081	1.8
Minnesota[c,d]	62,950	540	0.9	43,315	422	1.0
Mississippi[b]	22,030	3	--	19,496	3	--
Nebraska	14,513	84	0.6	10,557	98	0.9
North Dakota	13,900	950	6.8	6,900	750	10.9
South Carolina	84,284	1,272	1.5	65,360	948	1.5
Texas	243,329	688	0.3	247,102	776	0.3
Utah	176,137	1,030	0.6	144,645	728	0.5
Wyoming	3,817	93	2.4	2,552	76	3.0

Note: Applications include transfers and permits. Types of firearms included in a jurisdiction's checks or permits are described in *Jurisdiction notes*. For more information on reporting agencies and sample design, see *Methodology*.

--Less than 0.05%.

[a]Number of applications and denials was estimated for 2013. See *Methodology*.

[b]Number of denials was estimated. See *Methodology*.

[c]Totals for local agencies were compiled by a state agency.

[d]Permits are only exempt under state law. Other carry permits listed have a federal exemption.

Source: Bureau of Justice Statistics, Firearm Inquiry Statistics program, 2013 and 2014.

TABLE 4
Firearm applications received and denied by local agencies, by community size and type of permit, 2014

Population served	Applications	Denials	Percent denied
Purchase permits	289,080	11,548	4.0%
Population served			
9,999 or fewer	23,399	316	1.4%
10,000–99,999	119,177	4,724	4.0
100,000–199,999	67,658	2,360	3.5
200,000 or more	78,846	4,148	5.3
Exempt carry permits	359,207	4,247	1.2%
Population served			
9,999 or fewer	12,361	117	0.9%
10,000–99,999	153,905	1,747	1.1
100,000–199,999	87,128	1,468	1.7
200,000 or more	105,813	915	0.9

Note: Detail may not sum to total due to rounding. Counts are from agencies that provided data. For more information on reporting agencies and sample design, see *Methodology*. See appendix table 2 for standard errors.

Source: Bureau of Justice Statistics, Firearm Inquiry Statistics program, 2014.

TABLE 5
Reasons for denial of firearm transfer and permit applications, by checking agencies, 2013 and 2014

| Reason for denial | 2013 | | 2014 | | |
	FBI[a]	State	FBI[a]	State	Local
Total	100%	100%	100%	100%	100%
Felony indictment/charge	5.6%	3.5%	5.5%	8.7%	2.7%
Felony conviction	42.9	27.1	42.2	22.3	16.1
Felony arrest with no disposition	~	7.7	~	4.4	2.5
Fugitive from justice	18.2	12.9	19.1	10.8	3.2
Domestic violence misdemeanor	6.1	6.3	6.8	6.1	15.0
Domestic violence restraining order	3.1	5.5	2.9	4.9	4.7
Drug user/addict	10.4	3.7	10.4	5.3	4.6
Mental health commitment/adjudication	3.3	3.5	3.9	5.3	6.9
Illegal/unlawful alien	1.3	2.4	1.6	2.7	1.2
State law prohibition	8.8	23.9	7.3	25.7	19.9
Local law prohibition	/	/	/	/	2.3
Other prohibitions[b]	0.3	3.5	0.2	4.0	21.0

Note: Applications include transfers and permits. Reasons for denial were based on 18 U.S.C. § 922 and state laws. Totals were based on agencies that reported counts on reasons for denial. Local data are not available for 2013. For more information on reporting agencies and sample design, see *Methodology*. See appendix table 4 for counts.

~Not applicable. This is a not a federal disqualifier, but a disqualifer that is used in certain states.

/Not reported. This does not apply to the FBI or state agency reporters.

[a]During 2008, the FBI began a new classification system and reclassified all denials from 1999 to 2008. Therefore, totals are not comparable with those in editions of this report prior to 2008.

[b]Includes juveniles, persons dishonorably discharged from the U.S. Armed Forces, persons who have renounced U.S. citizenship, and other unspecified persons.

Sources: Bureau of Justice Statistics, Firearm Inquiry Statistics program, 2013 and 2014; and FBI, National Instant Criminal Background Check System Section Federal Denials, 2013 and 2014.

TABLE 6
Percent change in the number of applications, denials, and reasons for denial, 1999–2014

	1999	2014	Percent change, 1999–2014
Applications	8,621,000	14,993,000	73.9%
Denials[a]	204,000	193,000	-5.4%
Felony denials	148,000	82,000	-44.6
All other reasons	56,000	111,000	98.2
Percent felony[b]	72.5%	42.2%	~
Felony denials per 1,000 applications	17.2	5.5	~

Note: Applications include transfers and permits. Counts are rounded to the nearest 1,000. Annual counts may not sum to totals in other tables. Estimates were based on data reported by the FBI and state agencies that reported reasons for denial via the FIST program. Counts of some local agencies are included in the calculation for the distribution of felony denials. For more information on reporting agencies and sample design, see *Methodology*.

~Not applicable.

[a]During 2008, the FBI began a new classification system and reclassified all denials from 1999 to 2008. Therefore, totals are not comparable with those in editions of this report prior to 2008.

[b]The felony percentage is calculated from reported reasons for denial and is multiplied by the total number of denials to estimate the total number of felony denials.

Sources: Bureau of Justice Statistics, Firearm Inquiry Statistics program, 1999 and 2014; and FBI, National Instant Criminal Background Check System Background Checks—FBI Denials, 1999 and 2014.

TABLE 7
Bureau of Alcohol, Tobacco, Firearms and Explosives investigation of National Instant Criminal Background Check System denials by the FBI, 2013 and 2014

	2013		2014	
	Total	Percent	Total	Percent
FBI denials referred to ATF DENI Branch	93,993	100%	95,934	100%
DENI Branch referrals to ATF field divisions[a]				
Total referred to field	6,257	6.7%	7,978	8.3%
Delayed denials[b]	2,740	2.9	2,514	2.6
Standard denials[c]	3,517	3.7	5,464	5.7
Not referred to field	82,828	88.1%	83,440	87.0%
Not referred and overturned	4,858	5.2%	4,453	4.6%
Canceled[d]	50	0.1%	36	--
Awaiting response[e]	0	0.0%	27	--
Reasons for referrals to ATF field divisions				
Convicted felon	2,083	33.3%	2,917	36.6%
Subject to protective order	1,400	22.4	1,592	20.0
Domestic violence misdemeanor	1,042	16.7	1,434	18.0
Unlawful user of controlled substance	553	8.8	646	8.1
Fugitive from justice	430	6.9	536	6.7
Under indictment/information[f]	408	6.5	433	5.4
Adjudicated mentally defective	277	4.4	336	4.2
Illegal/unlawful alien	53	0.8	74	0.9
Career armed criminal	4	0.1	6	0.1
Dishonorable discharge	5	0.1	4	0.1
State prohibition	1	--	0	0.0
U.S. State Department subject	1	--	0	0.0

Note: Detail may not sum to total due to rounding.

--Less than 0.05%.

[a]A denial is referred if it is likely to merit prosecution under Bureau of Alcohol, Tobacco, Firearms and Explosives and U.S. Attorney criteria.

[b]A firearm may be obtained during an open transaction, where the FBI has not completed a check in 3 business days and the dealer is allowed to transfer the firearm. If the FBI completes the check and finds that the buyer is prohibited, a delayed denial referral is made to ATF.

[c]Involves a person who is not allowed to receive a firearm because the FBI found a prohibitory record within 3 business days.

[d]Represents NICS checks that should not have been conducted and were canceled by the FBI.

[e]DENI Branch specialist has contacted a court or law enforcement agency for additional information and is waiting for the results.

[f]An information is a formal accusation of a crime. It differs from an indictment because it is made by a prosecuting attorney rather than a grand jury.

Source: Bureau of Justice Statistics, based on data from Bureau of Alcohol, Tobacco, Firearms and Explosives, Denial Enforcement and NICS Intelligence Branch, Firearm Denial Statistics, 2013 and 2014.

Methodology

Data used for this report were prepared by the Regional Justice Information Service (REJIS) through a cooperative agreement with the Bureau of Justice Statistics (BJS) under the Firearm Inquiry Statistics (FIST) program. The FIST program collects information on background checks for firearm transfers or permits from federal, state, and local agencies.

FIST frame generation

State statutes determine which agencies conduct background checks for a firearm permit or transfer. To generate the FIST sampling frame for the 2014 collection, REJIS, under the direction of BJS, used multiple data sources combined with a large known pool of past FIST responders. First, REJIS included local agencies from the 2012 FIST frame that were known to have responded to the FIST survey at least once in the previous 3 years and had a verified status of conducting background checks or processing applications for firearm transfers or permits. REJIS used other data sources and resources to verify the frame, including the 2008 Census of State and Local Law Enforcement and a 2011 Originating Agency Identifier file of law enforcement agencies obtained from the FBI.

The 2014 FIST universe was composed of the following:

- **FBI**—30 states and the District of Columbia rely on the FBI's National Instant Criminal Background Check System (NICS) to conduct firearm background check activities for handguns and long gun transfers. In seven other states, the FBI's NICS conducts checks for long gun transfers only.

- **State reporting agencies**—31 state agencies and the District of Columbia police provide complete statewide counts of applications for firearm transfers or permits, denials of applications, and (when reported) reasons for denial for at least one type of check.

- **Local reporting agencies**—1,287 local checking agencies in 11 states issue permits, track applications and denials, or conduct background checks for various types of firearm permit or transfer systems.[3]

---

[3]The FIST program obtains data from local law enforcement agencies that conduct background checks and issue permits as well as from other types of local agencies that conduct these activities, such as probate courts (in Georgia) and county clerks or other types of administrative offices (in New York). In such cases, the agency surveyed may not actually conduct a background check but rather issue a permit, track a permit that was issued, or track a transfer check. For the FIST program, collecting application and denial data from agencies that conduct background checks or track permit or transfer applications is considered to be the most accurate and sometimes the only means available to assess background check activity. Additionally, populations covered by local agencies (for basic NICS checks and permits, not including other types of checks and permits, such as separate state-level checks and ATF-exempt carry permits) account for only 7% of the total U.S. population.

For the FIST program, it is important to distinguish between local agencies that are authorized by statute to conduct background checks and those that actually conduct the checks. Although local agencies in certain states are legally authorized to conduct background checks for firearm transfers or permits, these agencies are not required to do so. When developing the 2014 FIST frame, REJIS identified a few instances where a local agency (usually a municipal police department) that was legally authorized by state statute to conduct a background check had never actually conducted background check activities and was unlikely to ever do so. Instead, transfer or permit applicants who might use such a local agency are directed to another local authority (usually the county sheriff) with jurisdiction to conduct a transfer check or issue a permit. Agencies that did not conduct background check activities were considered to be out of scope for the 2014 data collection.

For the FIST data collection, BJS determined that eligible agencies in the frame should be those that are authorized to conduct and are known to conduct or maintain information on background checks. Such agencies collect or maintain data on the critical FIST data elements: applications, denials, and (when reported) the reasons for denial. Agencies that only have delegated background check functions are considered out of scope because they do not actually conduct firearm background check activities nor track information on such activities, which are the critical data collection items on the survey. Smaller law enforcement agencies that had closed since the construction of the FIST frame were determined to be out of scope for the 2014 data collection.

FIST sample

The 2014 FIST survey was designed to provide state-level estimates of background check activity. BJS produced a national estimate of the number of applications for firearms received and denied pursuant to the Brady Act by combining data obtained from state agencies and local checking agencies with FBI's NICS transaction data obtained from the FBI's NICS Section.[4]

REJIS collected state-level data from the state reporting agencies via survey or extracted publicly available online reports from the state website. Except for one state (Pennsylvania) in which denials were estimated, all data collected by state agencies are considered to be complete counts. To obtain FIST data in 2014, REJIS surveyed local agencies in 11 states with local checking agencies that were authorized to conduct firearm background check activities or process applications. Totals were estimated for states where the reporters were local agencies.

Local agencies in 8 (Idaho, Iowa, Montana, Nebraska, North Carolina, Nevada, New York, and West Virginia) of the 11 states were enumerated, and local agencies in 3 (Georgia, Minnesota, and Washington) of the states were sampled in 2 of the 4 sample strata due to the large number of potential reporters. REJIS created a stratified random sample proportionate to state and stratum size in each of the 3 states sampled based on population size that roughly equates to—

■ Stratum 1: rural—places of less than 10,000 population

■ Stratum 2: small cities—places of between 10,000 and 99,999 population

■ Stratum 3: small metropolitan areas—places of between 100,000 and 199,999 population

■ Stratum 4: large metropolitan areas—places of 200,000 or more population.

BJS created a reserve sample to account for potential low response rates for the 2014 collection. In total, a 30% reserve sample was drawn for each of the three sampled states; it was split into two reserve samples yielding a 15% sample per reserve sample. Because all agencies in strata 3 and 4 were surveyed, the reserve sample only affected strata 1 and 2

of the sampled agencies. The first reserve sample was to be used if one of the sampled states had a response rate of less than 85% for the initial data collection period. The second reserve sample was to be used if one of the sampled states had a response rate of less than 75% after the first reserve sample was collected. REJIS used the first and second reserve samples for Georgia in 2014. No reserve samples were used for the sampled agencies in Minnesota and Washington.

The final designated sample included 561 enumerated (self-representing or SR) local agencies and 274 sampled (non-self-representing or NSR) local agencies. After adjusting for agencies that were ineligible to participate in the survey, the final sample consisted of 845 state and local agencies. The overall response rate was 80%. All (100%) state agencies and 80% of local agencies responded to the survey (table 8).

BJS and REJIS updated the 2013–14 FIST survey form. To minimize respondent burden, the form was changed to provide clearer instructions tailored to terminology used by individual state agencies to describe the permit or permits of interest. BJS removed questions from the 2014 FIST survey on arrests, appeals, and reversals of denied applications because only a small number of agencies historically reported these data, which significantly limited the ability to draw reliable conclusions about the data. To increase survey response, REJIS used multiple survey modes (e.g., online form, paper survey, and fax) and a rigorous nonresponse follow-up contact strategy.

Estimation

Data obtained from state and local agencies were combined with the FBI's federal NICS transaction data to create an estimate of the total number of firearm transfer and permit applications received and denied nationally. REJIS applied design weights and nonresponse adjustment factors for enumerated and sampled local agencies to generate estimates of the number of applications and denials at the state level.

[4]The FBI reports on NICS transaction data in its annual *NICS Operations Report*. The FBI tracks the number of applications and denials processed by the NICS system. However, the FBI only reports reasons for denials made by the NICS Section and does not include reasons for denials issued at the state and local levels (information that FIST collects). In 2014, the FBI reported more than 12.7 million state Point of Contact transactions, compared to the approximately 6 million reported by FIST. This variation can be attributed to several factors, notably within the category of state firearm permits. The FIST counts include applications for two types of state firearm permits: (1) permits required for a transfer (purchase permits) and (2) concealed carry permits that may be used to exempt the holder from a background check at the time of transfer (exempt carry permits). At yearend 2014, 21 states had an exempt carry permit, and 29 other states had concealed carry permits that were not exempt and were not included in FIST. At least some of those 29 states used NICS for checks on applicants, and those checks have been included in the FBI statistics. The largest difference within the state firearm permit category was caused by periodic rechecks that at least two state agencies ran on all current carry permit holders. The rechecks were included in FBI transaction counts but not in FIST counts because they were not connected to a firearm transfer, and the FIST reporting agency was able to separately report new and renewed permit applications.

TABLE 8

Number of checking agencies in the 2014 Firearm Inquiry Statistics survey

Checking agencies	Total	Sample	Responses	Response rate
Total	1,319	845	679	80%
Statewide*	32	32	32	100%
Local	1,287	813	647	80%
Population served				
9,999 or fewer	574	289	223	77%
10,000–99,999	600	411	338	81
100,000–199,999	64	64	48	75
200,000 or more	49	49	38	78

Note: Agencies that were ineligible to participate in the FIST survey were deemed out of scope and removed from all counts of checking agencies.

*The same agencies were also surveyed for 2013 data. The response rate among state agency reporters for 2013 was 97% (31 responses).

Source: Bureau of Justice Statistics, Firearm Inquiry Statistics program, 2014.

The 2014 FIST data collection provides for two basic weighting structures for local respondent agencies: a weight applied to SR agencies and a weight applied to NSR agencies.

SR agencies (enumerated)

Each local checking agency within the eight states in which all known eligible agencies were contacted received a design weight of 1 (w1 = 1). In addition to the design weight, a nonresponse adjustment (w2) was applied to responding agencies to compensate for the agencies that did not respond.

NSR agencies (sampled)

The process for calculating weights for NSR agencies was similar to that for SR agencies, except these agencies (the small agencies in strata 1 and 2 of the sampled states) received a design weight of greater than 1 (w1 > 1) according to the population-based stratum and the state in which they reside. This weight reflects the inverse of the probability of selection for the state and stratum size (cell) in which the agency resides. The reserve samples for Minnesota and Washington were not released. In these cases, the design weights were further adjusted to compensate for the reserve subsampling. Agencies in strata 3 and 4 (large agencies) were selected with certainty and were therefore given a weight of 1. Weights were adjusted for any agencies that were out of scope in the sampled states.

Nonresponse adjustment

The nonresponse adjustment accounts for agencies that were ineligible (out of scope) and for nonrespondents. It consists of a ratio adjustment of the sum of the weighted eligible agencies (per state and population size stratum) to the sum of weighted respondent agencies (also per state and population size stratum). A nonresponse adjustment was applied to each cell (stratum within state) if there was any nonresponse. This created a specific adjustment for each cell that applies to all states, whether enumerated or sampled.

Partial-year reporting adjustment

A weight (w3), consisting of a small ratio adjustment to account for missing months of data, was applied to adjust for any agency that reported only partial-year data. This adjustment to account for missing months was necessary for six local agencies and to calculate reasons for denial from Pennsylvania.

Final weights

The final weights (Fw) applied to each FIST case are the product of a design weight applied to each agency, a nonresponse adjustment weight, and the partial-year reporting weight (Fw = w1 × w2 × w3).

Item nonresponse imputation for local agencies

For the 2014 FIST collection, REJIS determined that there were very few cases in which information on applications for firearm transfers or permits was missing. There were more cases of missing data for denials, but this was a small number compared to other missing data (e.g., reasons for denial). To count partial responses, agencies were required to report either the number of applications received or the number of denials issued. If neither was present, the agency was considered a nonrespondent. Fifteen agencies provided denials but not applications. Twenty-eight agencies provided the number of applications but not denials. In the instances of missing data on applications or denials, REJIS used a conditional mean imputation to estimate the number of applications and denials.

To yield the most reliable estimates, REJIS replaced missing values with the mean number of applications of other agencies in the same state that were in the same population category. In population stratum 1, this approach was deemed sufficient because all agencies served a population of less than 10,000. In population stratum 2, the population size covered a broad range (10,000 to 99,999). As such, a traditional group-mean replacement would have produced unacceptably imprecise approximations. To address this, for agencies with complete data, REJIS employed a basic multiple imputation strategy that took into account the number of denials, the actual population size served, and the number of applications to calculate the estimated number of applications in instances of missing data. The result was a within-state and stratum group-based sum of imputed values, but it was proportionate to the population allocation of imputed applications or denials per agency.

Estimates for 2013 data

BJS collected 2013 and 2014 data from federal agencies and from the 31 state agency reporters and the District of Columbia. Due to various factors, including time spent revising the survey to incorporate more accurate terminology familiar to respondents, complexities associated with trying to collect multiple years of data from local jurisdictions, and BJS's objective to report more timely FIST data, BJS collected only 2014 data from local checking agencies.[5] To account for the missing 2013 local agency data in the national estimate, REJIS used available FIST

---

[5]To mitigate reporting burden, BJS collected only 2014 data from local checking agencies. While state agencies are more likely to maintain the requested data in an automated format (e.g., a database), local agencies, especially those in smaller jurisdictions, may not have access to these same resources. These agencies may need to gather FIST data from files or other sources that require manual counts, and requesting multiple years of data could result in an unnecessary increase in respondent burden when reliable estimates can be produced in a different way.

2012, 2013, and 2014 state data to estimate the number of applications and denials from local agencies.[6] Specifically, REJIS used a random intercept linear regression spline model with one knot at 2013 to incorporate the hierarchical structure of the data (multiple time points and total application and denials estimates per state) to separately model total applications and total denials. The spline models were selected over conditional growth models (linear or quadratic) to allow for nonlinearity in the trends in total applications (and denials) over time across all states. To improve the overall imputations, these models also incorporated either a fixed or time varying covariate shown to be highly correlated with the FIST applications and denials totals over time.

Adjustments to data

REJIS obtained concealed carry permit data from Michigan by fiscal year, which were used to provide estimates for calendar years 2013 and 2014.

Mississippi reported applications for 2013 and 2014 but did not report denials for either year. Because sufficient data from prior years were unavailable to calculate an estimate using a linear trend, the ratio of denials to applications reported by Mississippi in 2012 was used to calculate a simple ratio that was applied to the number of applications to estimate the number of denials.

Pennsylvania reported the number of instant checks for 2013 and 2014, which are included in the FIST national estimate. The proportion of all Pennsylvania transactions that were instant checks was used to estimate the number of denials of instant checks and reasons for denials.

Standard errors

Standard error calculations were computed for the estimates of total applications, total denials, and the ratio of denials to total applications for three types: purchase, transfer and concealed carry permits across states, and size of region for local agencies. The standard error computations take into account several aspects of the FIST design, including stratification of data collection by a combination of state and population served categories and finite population sampling (without replacement) across the states and population categories of interest. REJIS approximated the FIST design by generating 68 final strata defined as combinations of state and population categories. Data from SR agencies were treated as certainty samples with an initial selection probability of one. For these states and population category combinations, complete responses would have a negligible contribution to the overall standard errors for a given estimate. To account for this and the fact that finite population correction (FPC) factors for the samples

generated by the FIST design were very small, FPCs were directly incorporated into the standard error computations. Finally, estimates for local agencies included one additional subdomain of agency type: local or state (centralized reporting). All computations were generated using the FIST final sampling weight, which incorporated adjustments for missing values, nonresponse, and an overall population eligibility or coverage adjustment. In some cases, standard error computations were not possible, as only one agency reported information from a given type of application in areas where more than one agency was queried (via sample or census). In these cases, no standard error computations were provided.

Reasons for denial

BJS has collected information about reasons for denial since the FIST program's inception in 1996. The FIST survey includes 12 categories that reflect the most common reasons for denial and closely match the categories of federal prohibitors. NICS POC agencies enforce federal prohibitors and state law prohibitors that may vary from the federal categories (see appendix table 6 for a list of federal and state prohibitors). Agencies that responded to the FIST survey were asked to record their denials in the most appropriate categories. When REJIS obtained data from an agency's website or internal report that did not match with an existing FIST denial category, REJIS determined which denial category best matched the reported reason and verified the classification with the responding agency.

In 2014, the FBI, 18 state agencies, and approximately 330 local agencies reported reasons for denials. There are two major difficulties in reporting reasons for denial.

First, among reporting agencies there was a high degree of nonresponse on items that asked about reasons for denial. Among local agencies, nonresponse was high in most states and population strata. Local agencies in one state (New York) did not report any reasons for denial. In 2014, the FBI and some state agencies provided a reason for each denial. Other state agencies provided reasons only for some denials, and some state agencies did not provide any reasons for denials.

Second, the method by which agencies record or track reasons for a denial varies among state and local agencies. Of those that report any reasons for a denial, approximately three-quarters of local agencies report all of the reasons found on a background check that disqualify a permit or transfer seeker from obtaining a firearm, while a quarter of agencies report only one reason for a denial. This proportion is reversed among state agencies, for which a third report all of the reasons a permit or transfer was denied and two-thirds report only one reason. Another difficulty among some state and local agencies that report one reason for a denial is that some report only the most serious charge listed

---

[6]Data were also estimated for the state agency reporter from Illinois, as data were not provided for 2013.

on a background check, others list the first reason found, and others do not indicate how they determined which reason to report.

Due to the high nonresponse and variation in the way reasons for denial are reported, a simple estimation for the number of reasons for denial by local agencies was calculated. Estimates used only the agency base weight rather than the final weight that was applied to all other local agency estimates. (See *Final weights* section.) This was done to bring the representation of responses from sampled agencies in line with those from states in which a census of agencies was conducted. The FBI and state agency reasons for denial counts are reported, and no estimation on these counts was conducted.

Definitions

Application for firearm transfer is information submitted by a person to a state or local checking agency to purchase a firearm or obtain a permit that can be used for a purchase. Information may be submitted directly to a checking agency or forwarded by a prospective seller.

Denial occurs when an applicant is prohibited from receiving a firearm or a permit that can be used to receive a firearm because a disqualifying factor was found during a background check.

Exempt carry permit is a state carry permit (issued after a background check) that exempts the holder from a check at the time of purchase under an ATF regulation or state law.

Federal Firearms Licensee (FFL) is also known as a federally licensed firearms dealer. A dealer must be licensed by the Bureau of Alcohol, Tobacco, Firearms and Explosives (ATF) to be classified as an FFL and must be enrolled with the FBI's NICS to request a NICS check.

Firearm is any weapon that is designed to or may readily be converted to expel a projectile by the action of an explosive.

Handgun is a firearm that has a short stock and is designed to be held and fired using a single hand, such as a pistol or revolver.

Instant check (instant approval) systems require a seller to transmit a purchaser's application to a checking agency by telephone or computer, after which the agency is required to respond as quickly as possible.

Long gun is a firearm with a barrel extended to about 30 inches to improve accuracy and range, commonly with a shoulder butt, and designed to be fired with two hands, such as a rifle or shotgun.

National Instant Criminal Background Check System (NICS) is a national system that checks available records to determine if prospective transferees are disqualified from receiving firearms.

Other approval systems require a seller to transmit a purchaser's application to a checking agency by telephone or other means. The agency is not required to respond immediately but must respond before the end of the statutory time limit.

Purchase permit systems require a prospective firearm purchaser to obtain, after a background check, a government-issued document (called a permit, license, or identification card) that must be presented to a seller to receive a firearm.

Transactions are inquiries to the federal NICS system and may include more than one inquiry per application.

Jurisdiction notes

The following notes provide additional information about changes in jurisdictions that occurred and about the types of firearms included in a jurisdiction's instant checks, purchase permits, exempt carry permits, or other approval checks in 2013 and 2014. Jurisdiction statutes should be consulted for complete details on a jurisdiction's firearm laws.

Alaska—A state agency conducted background checks on applicants for exempt carry permits that may have been used for handgun or long gun transfers.

Arizona—A state agency conducted background checks on applicants for exempt carry permits that may have been used for handgun or long gun transfers.

Arkansas—A state agency conducted background checks on applicants for exempt carry permits that may have been used for handgun or long gun transfers.

California—A state agency conducted other approval checks on applicants for handgun and long gun transfers.

Colorado—A state agency conducted instant checks on applicants for handgun and long gun transfers.

Connecticut—The state authorized two types of purchase permits, and every handgun transferee was required to obtain one of the permits. Beginning April 1, 2014, a purchase permit was also required for a long gun. In addition, a state agency conducted instant checks at the point of transfer on applicants for handgun and long gun transfers.

District of Columbia—The chief of police conducted checks on applicants for a registration certificate (categorized by the FIST as a purchase permit), which was required to obtain a handgun or a long gun. In addition, the FBI conducted NICS checks requested by dealers who transferred a firearm after receiving a buyer's registration certificate.

Florida—A state agency conducted instant checks on applicants for handgun and long gun transfers.

Georgia—Local agencies issued exempt carry permits that may have been used for handgun or long gun transfers.

Hawaii—A purchase permit was required to obtain a handgun or a long gun. Local agencies conducted checks on purchase permit applicants.

Idaho—Local agencies issued exempt carry permits that may have been used for handgun or long gun transfers.

Illinois—A purchase permit was required to obtain a handgun or a long gun. In addition, a state agency conducted instant checks at the point of transfer on applicants for handgun and long gun transfers.

Iowa—A purchase permit was required to obtain a handgun. An exempt carry permit may have been substituted for the purchase permit. Both types of permits may have been used to acquire a long gun. Local agencies conducted checks on applicants for purchase and exempt carry permits.

Kansas—A state agency conducted background checks on applicants for exempt carry permits that may have been used for handgun or long gun transfers.

Kentucky—A state agency conducted background checks on applicants for exempt carry permits that may have been used for handgun or long gun transfers.

Maryland—A purchase permit issued by a state agency was required to obtain a handgun after October 1, 2013. In addition, a state agency conducted other approval checks on applicants for transfers of handguns and assault weapons, which were designated by state law as regulated firearms.

Massachusetts—A purchase permit was required to obtain a handgun or a long gun. Three types of purchase permits were included in the FIST survey data. Local agencies conducted checks on permit applicants.

Michigan—A purchase permit was required for a handgun transfer between two individuals who were not licensed dealers. An exempt carry permit may have been substituted for the purchase permit and may have also been used to acquire a long gun. Local agencies conducted checks on purchase permit and exempt carry permit applicants.

Minnesota—A purchase permit was required to obtain a handgun or an assault weapon. An exempt carry permit may have been substituted for the purchase permit. Local agencies conducted checks on purchase and exempt carry permit applicants.

Mississippi—A state agency conducted background checks on applicants for exempt carry permits that may have been used for handgun or long gun transfers.

Montana—Local agencies issued exempt carry permits that may have been used for handgun or long gun transfers.

Nebraska—Local agencies conducted checks on applicants for a purchase permit, which was required to obtain a handgun. An exempt carry permit issued by a state agency may have been substituted for the purchase permit. Both types of permits may have been used to acquire a long gun.

Nevada—A state agency conducted instant checks on applicants for handgun and long gun transfers. Local agencies issued exempt carry permits that may have been used for handgun or long gun transfers.

New Hampshire—A state agency conducted instant checks on applicants for handgun transfers.

New Jersey—A purchase permit was required to obtain a handgun or a long gun. Local agencies and the state police conducted checks on purchase permit applicants. In addition, the state police conducted instant checks at the point of transfer on applicants for handgun and long gun transfers.

New York—The state's purchase permit was required to obtain a handgun and certain types of long guns. Local agencies conducted checks on purchase permit applicants.

North Carolina—A purchase permit was required to obtain a handgun. An exempt carry permit may have been substituted for the purchase permit. Both types of permits may have been used to acquire a long gun. Local agencies conducted checks on applicants for purchase and exempt carry permits.

North Dakota—A state agency conducted background checks on applicants for exempt carry permits that may have been used for handgun or long gun transfers.

Oregon—A state agency conducted instant checks on applicants for handgun and long gun transfers.

Pennsylvania—A state agency conducted instant checks on applicants for handgun and long gun transfers.

Rhode Island—Local agencies conducted other approval checks on applicants for handgun and long gun transfers.

South Carolina—A state agency conducted background checks on applicants for exempt carry permits that may have been used for handgun or long gun transfers.

Tennessee—A state agency conducted instant checks on applicants for handgun and long gun transfers.

Texas—A state agency conducted background checks on applicants for exempt carry permits that may have been used for handgun or long gun transfers.

Utah—A state agency conducted instant checks on applicants for handgun and long gun transfers, and conducted background checks on applicants for exempt carry permits.

Virginia—A state agency conducted instant checks on applicants for handgun and long gun transfers.

Washington—Local agencies conducted other approval checks on applicants for handgun transfers.

West Virginia—Local agencies issued exempt carry permits that may have been used for handgun or long gun transfers on or after June 4, 2014, when the permit was qualified by ATF as an alternative to the NICS transfer check.

Wisconsin—A state agency conducted instant checks on applicants for handgun transfers.

Wyoming—A state agency conducted background checks on applicants for exempt carry permits that may have been used for handgun or long gun transfers.

Related Publications

Background Checks for Firearm Transfers - Statistical Tables, 2012 (NCJ 247815, December 2014)

Background Checks for Firearm Transfers - Statistical Tables, 2010 (NCJ 238226, February 2013)

Background Checks for Firearm Transfers - Statistical Tables, 2009 (NCJ 231679, October 2010)

Background Checks for Firearm Transfers - Statistical Tables, 2008 (NCJ 227471, August 2009)

Background Checks for Firearm Transfers - Statistical Tables, 2007 (NCJ 223197, July 2008)

Background Checks for Firearm Transfers - Statistical Tables, 2006 (NCJ 221786, March 2008)

Background Checks for Firearm Transfers, 2005 (NCJ 214256, November 2006)

Background Checks for Firearm Transfers, 2004 (NCJ 210117, October 2005)

Background Checks for Firearm Transfers, 2003: Trends for the Permanent Brady Period, 1999–2003 (NCJ 204428, September 2004)

Background Checks for Firearm Transfers, 2002 (NCJ 200116, September 2003)

Background Checks for Firearm Transfers, 2001 (NCJ 195235, September 2002)

Background Checks for Firearm Transfers, 2000 (NCJ 187985, July 2001)

Background Checks for Firearm Transfers, 1999 (NCJ 180882, June 2000)

Data on this subject for the Brady Interim period prior to the permanent provisions are available in *Presale Handgun Checks, the Brady Interim Period, 1994–98* (NCJ 175034, June 1999)

Enforcement of the Brady Act, 2010: Federal and State Investigations and Prosecutions of Firearm Applicants Denied by a NICS Check in 2011
https://www.ncjrs.gov/pdffiles1/bjs/grants/239272.pdf

Enforcement of the Brady Act, 2009: Federal and State Investigations and Prosecutions of Firearm Applicants Denied by a NICS Check in 2009
https://www.ncjrs.gov/pdffiles1/bjs/grants/234173.pdf

Enforcement of the Brady Act, 2008: Federal and State Investigations and Prosecutions of Firearm Applicants Denied by a NICS Check in 2008
http://www.ncjrs.gov/pdffiles1/bjs/231052.pdf

Enforcement of the Brady Act, 2007: Federal and State Investigations and Prosecutions of Firearm Applicants Denied by a NICS Check in 2007
http://www.ncjrs.gov/pdffiles1/bjs/grants/227604.pdf

Enforcement of the Brady Act, 2006
http://www.ncjrs.gov/pdffiles1/bjs/grants/222474.pdf

Federal Firearms Cases, FY 2008
http://www.ncjrs.gov/pdffiles1/bjs/grants/229420.pdf

Federal Firearms Cases, FY 2007
http://www.ncjrs.gov/pdffiles1/bjs/grants/224890.pdf

Summary of State Firearm Transfer Laws, December 31, 2013
https://www.ncjrs.gov/pdffiles1/bjs/grants/248657.pdf

The following BJS surveys provide an overview of the firearm check procedures in each of the states and the states' interaction with NICS:

Survey of State Procedures Related to Firearm Sales, 2005 (NCJ 214645, November 2006)

Survey of State Procedures Related to Firearm Sales, Midyear 2004 (NCJ 209288, August 2005)

Survey of State Procedures Related to Firearm Sales, Midyear 2003 (NCJ 203701, August 2004)

Survey of State Procedures Related to Firearm Sales, Midyear 2002 (NCJ 198830, April 2003)

Survey of State Procedures Related to Firearm Sales, Midyear 2001 (NCJ 192065, April 2002)

Survey of State Procedures Related to Firearm Sales, Midyear 2000 (NCJ 186766, April 2001)

Survey of State Procedures Related to Firearm Sales, Midyear 1999 (NCJ 179022, March 2000)

Survey of State Procedures Related to Firearm Sales, 1997 (NCJ 173942, December 1998)

Survey of State Procedures Related to Firearm Sales, 1996 (NCJ 160705, September 1997)

Survey of State Procedures Related to Firearm Sales (NCJ 160763, May 1996)

The following BJS survey examines the quality and accessibility of certain criminal and noncriminal records when states conduct a firearm presale background check:

Survey of State Records Included in Presale Background Checks: Mental Health Records, Domestic Violence Misdemeanor Records, and Restraining Orders, 2003 (NCJ 206042, August 2004)

Trends for Background Checks for Firearm Transfers, 1999–2008
http://www.ncjrs.gov/pdffiles1/bjs/grants/231187.pdf

APPENDIX TABLE 1
Estimated standard errors for firearm applications received and denied by local agencies, 2014

	Applications	Denials	Percent denied
Total	19,265	731	0.07%
Purchase permits	13,860	678	0.20%
Exempt carry permits	7,957	171	0.04
Other approvals	7,658	56	0.04

Source: Bureau of Justice Statistics, Firearm Inquiry Statistics program, 2014.

APPENDIX TABLE 2
Standard errors for table 4: Firearm applications received and denied by local agencies, by community size and type of permit, 2014

	Applications	Denials	Percent denied
Purchase permits	13,860	678	0.20%
Population served			
9,999 or fewer	1,972	36	0.10%
10,000–99,999	5,904	245	0.30
100,000–199,999	5,902	184	0.30
200,000 or more	10,886	604	0.50
Exempt carry permits	7,957	171	0.04%
Population served			
9,999 or fewer	436	12	0.10%
10,000–99,999	4,274	115	0.10
100,000–199,999	3,528	106	0.10
200,000 or more	5,693	68	0.10

Source: Bureau of Justice Statistics, Firearm Inquiry Statistics program, 2014.

Firearm applications received and denied by jurisdiction, 2014

Jurisdiction	Applications	Standard error	Denials	Standard error	Percent denied	Standard error
Alaska						
Exempt carry	2,018	~	12	~	0.6%	~
Arizona						
Exempt carry	52,049	~	358	~	0.7%	~
Arkansas						
Exempt carry	41,725	~	920	~	2.2%	~
California						
Other approval	931,037	~	8,569	~	0.9%	~
Colorado						
Instant check	314,976	~	6,068	~	1.9%	~
Connecticut	133,364		112		0.1%	
Instant check	115,460	~	91	~	0.1	~
Purchase permit	17,904	~	21	~	0.1	~
District of Columbia						
Purchase permit	1,366	~	10	~	0.7%	~
Florida						
Instant check	774,363	~	11,372	~	1.5%	~
Georgia						
Exempt carry[a]	154,189	5,920	2,053	130	1.3%	0.1%
Hawaii						
Purchase permit	19,365	~	148	~	0.8%	~
Idaho						
Exempt carry[a]	28,248	1,716	134	13	0.5%	0.03%
Illinois	572,077		9,557		1.7%	
Instant check	401,899	~	1,616	~	0.4	~
Purchase permit	170,178	~	7,941	~	4.7	~
Iowa	43,836	834	1,161	144	2.6%	0.3%
Purchase permit[a]	16,170	296	835	140	5.2	0.9
Exempt carry[a]	27,666	556	326	9	1.2	0.0
Kansas						
Exempt carry	21,976	~	146	~	0.7%	~
Kentucky						
Exempt carry	31,889	~	560	~	1.8%	~
Maryland	44,939		597		1.3%	
Other approval	28,633	~	346	~	1.2	~
Purchase permit	16,306	~	251	~	1.5	~
Massachusetts						
Purchase permit	68,906	~	2,600	~	3.8%	~
Michigan	159,303		3,033		1.9%	
Purchase permit	43,702	~	952	~	2.2	~
Exempt carry	115,601	~	2,081	~	1.8	~
Minnesota[b]	100,081		1,439		1.4%	
Purchase permit[a]	56,766	5,359	1,017	80	1.8	0.2%
Exempt carry[c]	43,315	~	422	~	1.0	~
Mississippi						
Exempt carry	19,496	~	3	~	0.0%	~
Montana						
Exempt carry[a]	13,215	1,632	141	11	1.1%	0.1%
Nebraska[b]	41,030	~	887	~	2.2%	~
Purchase permit[a]	30,473	457	789	22	2.6	0.1%
Exempt carry	10,557	~	98	~	0.9	~
Nevada[b]	108,748	~	1,763	~	1.6%	~
Instant check	95,427	~	1,716	~	1.8	~
Exempt carry[a]	13,321	800	47	4	0.4	0.0%

Continued on next page

Firearm applications received and denied by jurisdiction, 2014

Jurisdiction	Applications	Standard error	Denials	Standard error	Percent denied	Standard error
New Hampshire						
Instant check	43,000	~	340	~	0.8%	~
New Jersey	169,715	~	1,282	~	0.8%	~
Instant check	95,267	~	464	~	0.5	~
Purchase permit	74,448	~	818	~	1.1	~
New York						
Purchase permit[a]	58,747	10,070	1,668	186	2.8%	0.4%
North Carolina	233,856	11,823	8,681	672	3.7%	0.2%
Purchase permit[a]	126,925	7,853	7,238	632	5.7	0.3
Exempt carry[a]	106,931	4,617	1,443	109	1.3	0.1
North Dakota						
Exempt carry	6,900	~	750	~	10.9%	~
Oregon						
Instant check	233,878	~	1,590	~	0.7%	~
Pennsylvania						
Instant check[a]	655,457	~	9,620	~	1.5%	~
Rhode Island						
Other approval	16,422	~	121	~	0.7%	~
South Carolina						
Exempt carry	65,360	~	948	~	-1.5%	~
Tennessee						
Instant check	428,017	~	17,832	~	-4.2%	~
Texas						
Exempt carry	247,102	~	776	~	0.3%	~
Utah	236,082	~	2,713	~	1.1%	~
Instant check	91,437	~	1,985	~	2.2	~
Exempt carry	144,645	~	728	~	0.5	~
Virginia						
Instant check	405,838	~	2,661	~	0.7%	~
Washington						
Other approval[a]	137,075	7,658	675	56	0.5%	0.0%
West Virginia						
Exempt carry[a,d]	15,636	636	104	8	0.7%	0.1%
Wisconsin						
Instant check	102,887	~	988	~	1.0%	~
Wyoming						
Exempt carry	2,552	~	76	~	3.0%	~

Note: For more information on reporting agencies and sample design, see *Methodology*. Types of firearms included in a jurisdiction's checks or permits are described in *Jurisdiction notes*.

~Not applicable. Complete counts were obtained and no sampling error is present.

[a]Totals were estimated (denials only for Pennsylvania).

[b]Standard errors not applicable to total because a portion of the estimate came from a state reporter.

[c]Permits are only exempt under state law. Other carry permits listed have a federal exemption.

[d]Totals are for June 4 to December 31, 2014.

Source: Bureau of Justice Statistics, Firearm Inquiry Statistics program, 2013.

APPENDIX TABLE 4
Firearm applications received and denied by jurisdiction, 2013

Jurisdiction	Applications	Denials	Percent denied	Jurisdiction	Applications	Denials	Percent denied
Alaska				**Mississippi**			
Exempt carry	1,774	12	0.7%	Exempt carry	22,030	3	0.0%
Arizona				**Nebraska**			
Exempt carry	71,104	364	0.5%	Exempt carry	14,513	84	0.6%
Arkansas				**Nevada**			
Exempt carry	58,699	431	0.7%	Instant check	120,891	1,908	1.6%
California				**New Hampshire**			
Other approval	960,179	7,493	0.8%	Instant check	50,700	350	0.7%
Colorado				**New Jersey**	229,719	2,556	1.1%
Instant check	396,955	7,351	1.9%	Instant check	123,553	620	0.5
Connecticut	201,294	270	0.1%	Purchase permit	106,166	1,936	1.8
Instant check	145,552	210	0.1	**North Dakota**			
Purchase permit	55,742	60	0.1	Exempt carry	13,900	950	6.8%
District of Columbia				**Oregon**			
Purchase permit	1,154	10	0.9%	Instant check	263,283	2,151	0.8%
Florida				**Pennsylvania**[a]			
Instant check	869,560	11,493	1.3%	Instant check	655,457	9,620	1.5%
Hawaii				**Rhode Island**			
Purchase permit	22,765	232	1.0%	Other approval	21,648	145	0.7%
Illinois[a]	829,930	8,341	1.0%	**South Carolina**			
Instant check	505,009	1,448	0.3	Exempt carry	84,284	1,272	1.5%
Purchase permit	324,921	6,893	2.1	**Tennessee**			
Kansas				Instant check	473,610	13,267	2.8%
Exempt carry	31,004	72	0.2%	**Texas**			
Kentucky				Exempt carry	243,329	688	0.3%
Exempt carry	58,706	1,098	1.9%	**Utah**	286,760	2,617	0.9%
Maryland	134,134	1,171	0.9%	Instant check	110,623	1,587	1.4
Other approval	129,359	1,125	0.9	Exempt carry	176,137	1,030	0.6
Purchase permit	4,775	46	1.0	**Virginia**			
Massachusetts				Instant check	479,253	2,412	0.5%
Purchase permit	125,491	3,144	2.5%	**Wisconsin**			
Michigan	188,731	2,890	1.5%	Instant check	135,013	1,117	0.8%
Purchase permit	58,831	1,228	2.1	**Wyoming**			
Exempt carry	129,900	1,662	1.3	Exempt carry	3,817	93	2.4%
Minnesota[b]							
Exempt carry	62,950	540	0.9%				

Note: For more information on reporting agencies and sample design, see *Methodology*. Types of firearms included in a jurisdiction's checks or permits are described in *Jurisdiction notes*.

[a]Totals were estimated (denials only for Pennsylvania).

[b]Permits are only exempt under state law. Other carry permits listed have a federal exemption.

Source: Bureau of Justice Statistics, Firearm Inquiry Statistics program, 2013.

Reasons for denial of firearm transfer and permit applications, by checking agencies, 2013 and 2014

Reason for denial	2013		2014		
	FBI[a]	State	FBI[a]	State	Local
Total	88,203	37,738	90,895	49,979	7,022
Felony indictment/charge	4,907	1,316	4,956	4,334	187
Felony conviction	37,843	10,228	38,379	11,126	1,133
Felony arrest with no disposition	~	2,922	~	2,179	179
Fugitive from justice	16,071	4,879	17,400	5,413	225
Domestic violence misdemeanor	5,342	2,375	6,190	3,034	1,052
Domestic violence restraining order	2,761	2,066	2,650	2,447	327
Drug user/addict	9,178	1,391	9,449	2,632	322
Mental health commitment/adjudication	2,932	1,336	3,557	2,650	484
Illegal/unlawful alien	1,121	898	1,431	1,325	81
State law prohibition	7,795	9,018	6,661	12,851	1,396
Local law prohibition	/	/	/	/	159
Other prohibitions[b]	253	1,309	222	1,988	1,477

Note: Applications include transfers and permits. Reasons for denial were based on 18 U.S.C. § 922 and state laws. Totals were based on agencies that reported counts on reasons for denial. Local data are not available for 2013. For more information on reporting agencies and sample design, see *Methodology*.

~Not applicable. This is a not a federal disqualifier, but a disqualifer that is used in certain states.

/Not reported. This does not apply to the FBI or state agency reporters.

[a]During 2008, the FBI instituted a new classification system and reclassified all denials from 1999 to 2008. Therefore, totals are not comparable with those in editions of this report prior to 2008.

[b]Includes juveniles, persons dishonorably discharged from the U.S. Armed Forces, persons who have renounced U.S. citizenship, and other unspecified persons.

Sources: Bureau of Justice Statistics, Firearm Inquiry Statistics program, 2013 and 2014; and FBI, National Instant Criminal Background Check System Section Federal Denials, 2013 and 2014.

Prohibited person records in the National Instant Criminal Background Check System Index, 2014

| Type of record | January 1, 2014 | | | December 31, 2014 | | | |
| | Total | Submissions | | Total | Submissions | | Percent change |
		Federal	State*		Federal	State*	
Total	11,166,690	6,893,076	4,273,614	12,881,223	7,721,667	5,159,556	15.4%
Felony conviction	1,647,906	966,413	681,493	1,889,892	1,021,660	868,232	14.7%
Under indictment/information	34,222	33,791	431	32,975	32,439	536	-3.6
Fugitive from justice	392,138	6,012	386,126	469,578	6,676	462,902	19.7
Drug user/addict	33,909	16,160	17,749	24,281	12,527	11,754	-28.4
Mental health commitment/ adjudication	3,260,730	191,458	3,069,272	3,774,301	235,998	3,538,303	15.8
Illegal/unlawful alien	5,621,440	5,621,373	67	6,346,095	6,346,012	83	12.9
Dishonorable discharge	10,328	10,295	33	10,524	10,486	38	1.9
Renounced U.S. citizenship	23,807	23,794	13	27,240	27,220	20	14.4
Protection/restraining order	5,321	223	5,098	47,296	273	47,023	788.9
Misdemeanor domestic violence	93,812	21,582	72,230	112,799	23,030	89,769	20.2
Federally denied persons	33,005	0	33,005	30,285	0	30,285	-8.2
State law prohibition	10,072	1,975	8,097	115,957	5,346	110,611	1,051.3

Note: The NICS Index is used exclusively for NICS checks and contains records of persons who are prohibited by federal or state law from receiving or possessing a firearm. For more information on reporting agencies and sample design, see *Methodology*.

*State totals include U. S. territories.

Source: FBI, National Instant Criminal Background Check System Index, 2014.

Prohibited person records in the National Instant Criminal Background Check System Index, 2013

| Type of record | January 1, 2013 | | | December 31, 2013 | | | |
| | Total | Submissions | | Total | Submissions | | Percent change |
		Federal	State*		Federal	State*	
Total	8,323,931	5,526,483	2,797,448	11,166,690	6,893,076	4,273,614	34.2%
Felony conviction	727,255	79,940	647,315	1,647,906	966,413	681,493	126.6%
Under indictment/information	865	505	360	34,222	33,791	431	3,856.3
Fugitive from justice	378,463	3,834	374,629	392,138	6,012	386,126	3.6
Drug user/addict	18,174	11,186	6,988	33,909	16,160	17,749	86.6
Mental health commitment/ adjudication	1,821,217	161,813	1,659,404	3,260,730	191,458	3,069,272	79.0
Illegal/unlawful alien	5,216,732	5,216,675	57	5,621,440	5,621,373	67	7.8
Dishonorable discharge	10,163	10,135	28	10,328	10,295	33	1.6
Renounced U.S. citizenship	20,654	20,649	5	23,807	23,794	13	15.3
Protection/restraining order	4,101	198	3,903	5,321	223	5,098	29.7
Misdemeanor domestic violence	90,199	20,306	69,893	93,812	21,582	72,230	4.0
Federally denied persons	34,746	1	34,745	33,005	0	33,005	-5.0
State law prohibition	1,362	1,241	121	10,072	1,975	8,097	639.5

Note: The NICS Index is used exclusively for NICS checks and contains records of persons who are prohibited by federal or state law from receiving or possessing a firearm. For more information on reporting agencies and sample design, see *Methodology*.

*State totals include U. S. territories.

Source: FBI, National Instant Criminal Background Check System Index, 2013.

Reasons for denial of firearm transfer and permit applications, December 31, 2014

Jurisdiction	Felony[a]	Misdemeanor[b]	Fugitive from justice	Mental health commitment/ adjudication[c]	Court order[d]	Drug user/ addict[e]	Alcohol abuse[e]	Minor age	Juvenile offense	Unlawful/ illegal alien[f]
Federal	X	X	X	X	X	X	~	X	~	X
District of Columbia	X	X	~	X	X	X	X	X	~	~
State	49	28	15	34	31	31	19	49	27	17
Alabama	X	~	~	X	~	X	X	X	~	~
Alaska	X	~	~	~	X	X	X	X	X	~
Arizona	X	X	~	X	~	~	~	X	X	X
Arkansas	X	~	~	X	X	~	~	X	~	~
California	X	X	~	X	X	X	~	X	X	~
Colorado	X	~	~	~	~	~	~	X	X	~
Connecticut	X	X	~	X	X	~	~	X	X	X
Delaware	X	X	X	X	X	X	X	X	X	~
Florida	X	X	~	X	X	X	X	X	X	~
Georgia	X	X	~	~	~	~	~	X	X	~
Hawaii	X	X	X	X	X	X	X	X	X	X
Idaho	X	~	~	~	~	~	~	X	~	~
Illinois	X	X	~	X	X	X	~	X	X	X
Indiana	X	X	~	X	X	X	X	X	X	~
Iowa	X	X	~	~	X	~	~	X	X	~
Kansas	X	~	~	X	~	X	X	X	X	~
Kentucky	X	~	~	~	~	~	~	X	X	~
Louisiana	X	X	~	~	X	~	~	X	~	~
Maine	X	~	~	X	X	~	~	X	X	~
Maryland	X	X	X	X	X	X	X	X	X	~
Massachusetts	X	X	X	X	X	X	X	X	X	X
Michigan	X	X	~	X	X	~	~	X	~	X
Minnesota	X	X	X	X	X	X	~	X	X	X
Mississippi	X	~	~	~	~	X	X	X	~	~
Missouri	X	~	X	X	~	X	X	X	~	~
Montana	X	X	~	~	X	~	~	X	~	~
Nebraska	X	X	X	~	X	~	~	X	~	~
Nevada	X	~	X	X	X	X	~	X	~	X
New Hampshire	X	~	~	~	X	X	-	X	~	~
New Jersey	X	X	~	X	X	X	X	X	X	~
New Mexico	X	~	~	~	~	~	~	X	~	~
New York	X	X	X	X	X	X	~	X	~	X
North Carolina	X	~	X	X	X	X	~	X	~	X
North Dakota	X	X	~	X	~	~	~	X	~	~
Ohio	X	~	X	X	~	X	X	X	X	~
Oklahoma	X	~	~	X	~	X	X	X	X	~
Oregon	X	X	X	X	~	~	~	X	X	~
Pennsylvania	X	X	X	X	X	X	X	X	X	X
Rhode Island	X	~	X	X	X	X	~	X	~	X
South Carolina	X	~	X	X	~	X	X	X	~	X
South Dakota	X	X	~	~	~	X	~	X	~	~
Tennessee	X	X	~	X	X	X	X	X	~	~
Texas	X	X	~	~	X	X	X	X	~	~
Utah	X	~	~	X	~	X	~	X	X	X
Vermont	~	~	~	~	~	~	~	X	~	~
Virginia	X	X	~	X	X	X	~	X	X	X
Washington	X	X	~	X	X	X	~	X	X	X

Continued on next page

Reasons for denial of firearm transfer and permit applications, December 31, 2014

Jurisdiction	Felony[a]	Misdemeanor[b]	Fugitive from justice	Mental health commitment/ adjudication[c]	Court order[d]	Drug user/ addict[e]	Alcohol abuse[e]	Minor age	Juvenile offense	Unlawful/ illegal alien[f]
West Virginia	X	X	~	X	X	X	X	X	~	X
Wisconsin	X	~	~	X	X	~	~	X	X	~
Wyoming	X	~	~	~	~	~	~	~	~	~

Note: Federal prohibitors in 18 U.S.C. § 922 are the minimum standard nationwide. Table does not show state laws that incorporate federal prohibitions. A jurisdiction may have other prohibitions not listed in the table. Types of firearms, offenses, and dispositions covered by statutes vary by jurisdiction. See *Jurisdiction notes*.

X Indicates a basis under the jurisdiction's laws for prohibition of firearm transfers or possession or for denial of a permit required for a firearm transfer. Concealed carry permit restrictions are not included.

~Not applicable.

[a]An offense with a penalty of imprisonment for 1 year or more or designated a felony by law.

[b]An offense with a penalty of incarceration for less than 1 year or designated a misdemeanor by law. Includes domestic violence offenses and other offenses.

[c]Includes adjudications of mental illness or incapacity and involuntary or voluntary commitments for inpatient or outpatient mental health treatment.

[d]An order to prevent domestic violence, witness intimidation, stalking, or other criminal acts.

[e]A substance-related conviction, addiction to a substance, or intoxication during a firearm transfer.

[f]An illegal alien or a non-U.S. citizen not entitled to an exception that allows firearm possession.

Source: Bureau of Justice Statistics, Firearm Inquiry Statistics program, 2014.

APPENDIX TABLE 9
Agencies conducting firearm background checks, December 31, 2014

Jurisdiction	Name or description of checking agencies	
	Purchase check or permit	Exempt carry permit[a]
United States	Federal Bureau of Investigation	---
Alabama	---	---
Alaska	---	Department of Public Safety
Arizona	---	Department of Public Safety
Arkansas	---	State police
California	Department of Justice Firearms Division	---
Colorado	Bureau of Investigation Insta-Check Unit	---
Connecticut	State Police Special Licensing & Firearms	---
Delaware	---	---
District of Columbia	Metropolitan Police Department	---
Florida	Department of Law Enforcement	---
Georgia	---	County probate courts
Hawaii	Police departments	---
Idaho	---	County sheriffs
Illinois	State Police Firearm Owners Identification and Firearm Inquiry Transfer Program units	---
Indiana	---	---
Iowa	County sheriffs	Department of Public Safety / county sheriffs
Kansas	---	Attorney general
Kentucky	---	State police
Louisiana	---	---
Maine	---	---
Maryland	State Police Licensing Division	---
Massachusetts	Police departments	---
Michigan	Sheriffs and police departments	County licensing boards
Minnesota	Sheriffs and police departments	County sheriffs
Mississippi	---	Department of Public Safety
Missouri	---	---
Montana	---	County sheriffs
Nebraska	Sheriffs and police departments	State patrol
Nevada	Department of Public Safety	County sheriffs
New Hampshire	Department of Safety	---
New Jersey	State police /local police departments	---
New Mexico	---	---
New York[b]	Sheriffs and police departments	---
North Carolina	County sheriffs	County sheriffs
North Dakota	---	Bureau of Criminal Investigation
Ohio	---	---
Oklahoma	---	---
Oregon	State Police Firearms Unit	---
Pennsylvania	State Police Firearms Division	---
Rhode Island	Police departments	---
South Carolina	---	Law Enforcement Division
South Dakota	---	---
Tennessee	Bureau of Investigation Tennessee Instant Check System Unit	---
Texas	---	Department of Public Safety
Utah	Bureau of Criminal Identification	Bureau of Criminal Identification
Vermont	---	---
Virginia	State Police Firearms Transaction Program	---
Washington	Sheriffs and police departments	---
West Virginia	---	County sheriffs
Wisconsin	Department of Justice Firearms Unit	---
Wyoming	---	Attorney general

--- FBI conducts purchase checks or jurisdiction has no exempt permits.

[a]Agencies listed issue carry permits that may be used to waive a purchase check.

[b]License required for purchase may also allow carrying.

Source: Bureau of Justice Statistics, Firearm Inquiry Statistics program, 2014.

National Instant Criminal Background Check System checking agencies, FBI, or state Point of Contact for firearm transfers, 2014

State	FBI conducts checks for all firearms[a]	POC conducts checks for all firearms	POC checks handguns FBI checks long guns	State	FBI conducts checks for all firearms[a]	POC conducts checks for all firearms	POC checks handguns FBI checks long guns
Total	30	13	7	Montana	X	~	~
Alabama	X	~	~	Nebraska[b]	~	~	X
Alaska	X	~	~	Nevada	~	X	~
Arizona	X	~	~	New Hampshire	~	~	X
Arkansas	X	~	~	New Jersey	~	X	~
California	~	X	~	New Mexico	X	~	~
Colorado	~	X	~	New York	X	~	~
Connecticut	~	X	~	North Carolina[b]	~	~	X
Delaware	X	~	~	North Dakota	X	~	~
Florida	~	X	~	Ohio	X	~	~
Georgia	X	~	~	Oklahoma	X	~	~
Hawaii[b]	~	X	~	Oregon	~	X	~
Idaho	X	~	~	Pennsylvania	~	X	~
Illinois	~	X	~	Rhode Island	X	~	~
Indiana	X	~	~	South Carolina	X	~	~
Iowa[b]	~	~	X	South Dakota	X	~	~
Kansas	X	~	~	Tennessee	~	X	~
Kentucky	X	~	~	Texas	X	~	~
Louisiana	X	~	~	Utah	~	X	~
Maine	X	~	~	Vermont	X	~	~
Maryland	~	~	X	Virginia	~	X	~
Massachusetts	X	~	~	Washington[b]	~	~	X
Michigan	X	~	~	West Virginia	X	~	~
Minnesota	X	~	~	Wisconsin	~	~	X
Mississippi	X	~	~	Wyoming	X	~	~
Missouri	X	~	~				

Note: Includes checks on purchases or on permits required for purchase.

X Indicates agency conducting background checks.

~Not applicable.

[a]The FBI also conducts all National Instant Criminal Background Check System checks for American Samoa, the District of Columbia, Guam, Northern Mariana Islands, Puerto Rico, and the U.S. Virgin Islands.

[b]States with multiple Points of Contact.

Source: Bureau of Justice Statistics, Firearm Inquiry Statistics program, 2014.

APPENDIX TABLE 11
Forums for appeals of firearm transfer and permit denials, 2014

Jurisdiction	Denying agency	Other agency	Court system	Jurisdiction	Denying agency	Other agency	Court system
Federal				**Mississippi**			
Instant check	X	~	X	Exempt carry	X	~	X
Alaska				**Montana**			
Exempt carry	X	~	~	Exempt carry	~	~	X
Arizona				**Nebraska**			
Exempt carry	X	~	X	Purchase permit	~	~	X
Arkansas				Exempt carry	X	~	X
Exempt carry	X	~	X	**Nevada**			
California				Instant check	X	~	~
Other approval	X	~	~	Exempt carry	~	~	X
Colorado				**New Hampshire**			
Instant check	X	~	~	Instant check	X	~	X
Connecticut				**New Jersey**			
Instant check	X	~	~	Instant check	X	~	~
Purchase permit	~	X	~	Purchase permit	~	~	X
District of Columbia				**North Carolina**			
Purchase permit	X	~	X	Purchase permit	~	~	X
Florida				Exempt carry	~	~	X
Instant check	X	~	~	**North Dakota**			
Georgia				Exempt carry	X	~	X
Exempt carry	~	~	X	**Oregon**			
Idaho				Instant check	X	~	~
Exempt carry	~	~	X	**Pennsylvania**			
Illinois				Instant check	X	X	X
Instant check	X	~	X	**South Carolina**			
Purchase permit	X	~	X	Exempt carry	X	~	~
Iowa				**Tennessee**			
Purchase permit	~	~	X	Instant check	X	~	~
Exempt carry	~	~	X	**Texas**			
Kansas				Exempt carry	~	~	X
Exempt carry	X	X	X	**Utah**			
Kentucky				Instant check	X	~	~
Exempt carry	X	~	X	Exempt carry	~	X	~
Maryland				**Virginia**			
Other approval	X	~	X	Instant check	X	~	X
Purchase permit	X	~	X	**Washington**			
Massachusetts				Other approval	~	~	X
Purchase permit	~	~	X	**Wisconsin**			
Michigan				Instant check	X	~	X
Purchase permit	~	~	X	**Wyoming**			
Exempt carry	~	~	X	Exempt carry	X	~	X
Minnesota							
Purchase permit	~	~	X				
Exempt carry	X	~	X				

X Indicates statute or regulation provides a specific procedure to appeal a denial of a firearm transfer or permit. In addition, some denying agencies may reconsider a decision even if not required to do so by law.
~Not applicable.
Source: Bureau of Justice Statistics, Firearm Inquiry Statistics program, 2014.

The Bureau of Justice Statistics (BJS) of the U.S. Department of Justice is the principal federal agency responsible for measuring crime, criminal victimization, criminal offenders, victims of crime, correlates of crime, and the operation of criminal and civil justice systems at the federal, state, tribal, and local levels. BJS collects, analyzes, and disseminates reliable and valid statistics on crime and justice systems in the United States, supports improvements to state and local criminal justice information systems, and participates with national and international organizations to develop and recommend national standards for justice statistics. Jeri M. Mulrow is acting director.

The Regional Justice Information Service (REJIS) prepared these tables under the supervision of Allina D. Lee of BJS. Allen Beck, Ph.D., of BJS provided statistical consultation. Trent D. Buskirk, Ph.D., of REJIS provided statistical and sample design consultation. The tables were prepared under BJS cooperative agreement #2011-BJ-CX-K017. The BJS-sponsored Firearm Inquiry Statistics program collects information on firearm background checks conducted by state and local agencies and combines this information with Federal Bureau of Investigation National Instant Criminal Background Check System transaction data to create a national estimate of the number of applications received and denied annually pursuant to the Brady Handgun Violence Prevention Act of 1993 and similar state laws.

Morgan Young edited the report. Barbara Quinn produced the report.

June 2016, NCJ 249849

www.ingramcontent.com/pod-product-compliance
Lightning Source LLC
Chambersburg PA
CBHW081810280526
45789CB00008B/3072